THE MACMILLAN COMPANY
NEW YORK · BOSTON · CHICAGO · DALLAS
ATLANTA · SAN FRANCISCO

MACMILLAN & CO., LIMITED
LONDON · BOMBAY · CALCUTTA
MELBOURNE

**THE MACMILLAN COMPANY
OF CANADA, LIMITED**
TORONTO

More Than Bread

A BOOK OF POEMS

By

JOSEPH AUSLANDER

New York

THE MACMILLAN COMPANY

1936

PRINTED IN THE UNITED STATES OF AMERICA
BY THE STRATFORD PRESS, INC., NEW YORK

To

OTIS AND "JO"

The mind knows too much,
Breeding a barren art;
Wisdom, abhorring such,
Inhabits the heart.

Contents

MORE THAN BREAD

Soliloquy in the Grove

The sultry cicalas in your citron trees
Clash gongs and cymbals of impossible brass;
The hot noon throbs with their monotonies,
And seems, because of these,
Insufferably hotter than it was
When, side by side with Plato, you would pass
Along the luxurious margins of soft grass,
Cooling the corybantic revelries
Of worse than wasps or bees,
In silvery fountains of the spirit's singular felicities.

O bandy-legged and beloved ghost,
The limpid fervour of whose mind to some
Is bread and honeycomb;
Relentless nectar of the locust, bitter
As blood or salt, the pure and sunny frost
Of inquisition like the wasp's, but neater—
If only once again your lemon trees
Could hear that caustic tongue;
If only muddled times among,
Ours, alas, the most,
Your passion for cold truth, O Socrates,
Could penetrate. . . .
Faugh! there is nothing now save garrulous folly,
And settled melancholy,
And hate,
And the despot hammering loudly at the gate!

You could have asked one question at the close
To jolt Zeus upright like some drunken jailer
(Whom Death cheats with a duplicate set of keys) ;
But like that equally bald and garrulous sailor,
Whose wife's tongue drove him headlong to the
      wars,
You knew a neater way of opening doors.

Which was, to drink Zeus under the table first,
As at the Banquet Alcibiades,
Muddled between his throat's and his mind's thirst,
Snored with his massive head between his knees :
So sprawls Zeus in a stupor on the floor,
The key locked in the cup of hellebore.

There is your exit; not the obvious keys
That girdle the god's belly whose great snores
Clank them at every heave : Ah, Socrates,
Such suit Olympian louts and senators;
Not you, whose starry logic well disdains
The chain of keys, the key of endless chains.

No, hemlock is the horse whereon you ride,
Not unlike that proud other to whose wings
You added many a plume to match his pride;
No, hemlock is the horse for crownless kings,
The very mount for kings whose crown is only
The iron privilege of remaining lonely.

You might have said so much; there were so many
Things you might have said; you might have said
Any one of a hundred speeches, any
Of those profound futilities of the dead.
None of which suited you; you chose instead
To remember a debt, to pay the final penny.

From dawn to dusk you talked incessantly
According to your wont, as though you were
Walking the groves of the Academy
With Plato under the olives' silvery blur,
Walking and talking like a philosopher,
Talking and walking like some divinity.

And so you talked, all preparations made,
Bathed, in clean linen, rite and office done;
And so you talked to rouse, rebuke, persuade
As calmly as you faced the setting sun :
As when at Delium's bloody rout no one
But you walked that confusion unafraid.

And having bade the women of your house
Farewell, and sent them, lest they weep, away,
You drained your cup as at some brave carouse,
And said to Crito, "Crito, a debt's to pay."
And he, "What else?" "I have no more to say;
We owe a cock to Aesculapius."

You might have said. . . . What could you have said
  more?
You did not say it, being just and wise;
And what heroics, what fine metaphor
Could seem but brash and windy sophistries?
Come, close the mouth and cover up the eyes
And draw the decent sheet and shut the door.

The Aspen

I.

Brief summer of the aspen bowed,
No sorrow broods upon your leaf;
Your laughter shakes no bell; no shroud
Commemorates your grief.

These being vices of our kind
Wherewith our follies would infect
Beauty impersonal and blind,
Strength heedless and erect.

We cannot know these : neither blood
Nor purpose knits them to our bones.
They leave us to our brotherhood
Of barren sticks and stones.

They need no sign from us; they need
No part in our poor victory :
Not even when we nail our creed
Spread-eagled to a tree.

II.

I am the tree your axes chopped
To give your god a place.
Against my boughs His feet you propped;
I held His head a space;
The sweat poured down His face.

I am the tree you tore apart
Even in summer's bloom.
You nailed His heart against my heart
To mark our double doom.
I gave your god a room.

You cut me off from cloud and sun,
From water, root, and air,
That so the mischief you had done
Might climb as on a chair
To hang Him by the hair.

You cheated me of brood and nest;
You choked off song and bird
To give His broken body rest;
But of His cry one word
You could not hear; I heard.

The Hunger of the Word

I.

Whether he goes into a room where people
Make a great noise of nothing and cluck and cackle;
Or whether, some rainy dawn, he hears the grackle
Nailing a new roof to his dripping steeple:
The hunger of the word forever haunts him,
Nags at his bowels, bothers in his brain—
A shadow running beside him in the rain,
Something he needs and wants, something that
    wants him.
He cups his hand over an urgent anguish;
He warms it like a worm, a cold small clamour;
He breathes on it until he can faintly distinguish
A fog of gradual light beginning to glimmer,
Beginning to gather and glow, to pulse and expand,
To beat like a heart in the hollow of his hand.

II.

He holds the word like fire in his hand;
His hand is filled with fire, his flesh is bright;
His heart drinks from that rosy cup of light
A strength it cannot wholly understand,
This glowworm of the word, this luminous cheat,
Cupped in its pleasant and precarious nest,
Coaxed, by the warmth of love made manifest,
Gives back in light the duller gift of heat.
Thus out of men and women and talk and birds,
Wet streets and chilly mornings and the terror
Of his own heart and the confusion of words
The poet sees one cloudy word grow clearer
And put on light and make a Holy Land,
The god safe in the hollow of his hand.

Feet of Clay

Your forehead cannot frighten,
Your mouth does not dismay:
These will darken or brighten
The night, the day;
Only my knuckles whiten
Around your feet of clay.

Your golden forehead flashes,
Your mouth is grave and sweet;
Yet none of these abashes
With light, with heat:
Only my whole world crashes
But for your crumbling feet.

I would entreat you, alter,
If alter you must, in these:
The forehead whose flame can falter,
The mouth that can freeze:
But never relax the halter
That binds me to your knees.

Ah, never stiffen with splendour
Of gold or godlike disdain
The weakness to which I surrender,
The strength I cannot attain,
The clay that is human and tender
And friendly to pain.

The God

The god whose bones
Cannot stay bound,
Who pushes stones
And stars around,
And is not found

Anywhere beneath
Lock and key,
But blows like breath,
But stands a tree
Straight over me:

That is the god
Whose hand I trust:
Himself no clod,
He will not thrust
Me into dust.

Confucius moulders
In his tomb;
But this god smoulders,
The world for whom
Is narrow room;

For whom heaven
Is no vast place;
But the heart, even
One heart's slight grace,
Sufficient space.

In the heart only
His heart will not bleed:
No longer lonely,
No more in need
Of being a creed,

Of being a king
With secrets to keep,
Or anything,
He breathes deep,
He thinks of sleep.

As a child will stare
In drowsy surprise,
And rumple his hair
And rub his eyes—
So this god sighs,

So sleeps, who finds
The heart his home:
Familiar the blinds,
Chair, table become,
The pleasant gloom.

Wherefore the slow
Warm little smile
Will come and go
As dreams beguile
The god a while.

Easter Sunday

A man steps from his hiding place;
He feels the wind, he feels the sun;
He laughs and falls upon his face;
He weeps : and I am such a one.

He sees the happy children play;
He hears the happy children shout. . . .
A man walks out a little way;
He trembles as he walks about.

The pigeons patter from the boughs;
Like plums they drop into the grass;
The man turns back to his own house;
He stops to let the pigeons pass.

The hot sun fastens to his neck;
That lovely leech bites numb and sweet;
The fractured gusts of gold light fleck
The bleeding hands, the broken feet.

A man walks with averted face
Out of the glowing wind, the sun;
He pulls the stone back into place;
He weeps : and I am such a one.

The Vigil

I, watching for the first sign of a leaf,
The misty esperanto of the spring,
The soft green shout as instant and as brief
As a wing,
As grief;
I, watching all night for the pure pristine
Announcement of green,
Heard nothing, saw nothing of that miracle save
As Mary and His Mother at the grave,
Huddled through the long night, through the black
      horror
Of hope held strangling in the coils of error,
Still clung to that impossible hope
Until at length they heard,
As one might hear a bird
Hammering faintly at its shell,
The blood-caked fingers grope,
The bandages that fell,
The feet drag out of hell—
And could not look where they lay prone,
But knew it was their own,
But saw, as though love made a brilliant mirror,
That tallness of the lover and the son
Tottering over them both,
And yet were loath
To look, albeit they felt that it were sweet
To touch His feet;
Even to touch the nail
Still fastened in the bone.

So felt I, watching in the night, alone,
Aware of some strange shadow like a stone
Edging from off the heart, being tugged and shifted
Until it suddenly lifted,
And I could breathe and confidently knew
The night had risen too,
And the heaviness of winter also risen,
And the faint leaf stumbling blindly from its
     prison. . .

Not to the eyes that gaze, however hard,
Not to the eyes that stare,
The over-anxious ear,
Comes the incredible reward;
But only to the heart that feels the sign is there,
Yet does not dare
To look, lest April prove too fair,
Too sweet—
Having plucked April on a spring night and put it in
     one's hair,
Having once, long ago, washed those beautiful
     tortured feet.

The Pioneer

You will observe my blood on the stones
And my blood in the hollow,
And you will come after; there will be bones
For you to follow.

I found my father's bones on the trail,
Bleached white with the weather:
Though he had failed, I could not fail
Him altogether.

As he found his father's before him I found
His blood on the bush:
And I felt that I stood on Holy Ground
In a grim hush.

You must come after and give a name
To the nameless one
Who perished here that the bush might flame
Some day for his son.

Person from Porlock

Who was the man from Porlock?
Who blundered on Kublai Khan?
Did he wear a wet little forelock?
Was he a slippery warlock?
What sort of man was this man?

Was he that Tartar lord?
Or his Tartar architect
Who, when the minaret soared,
When the pleasure dome rose erect,
Was quieted with a cord?

Was he the world of prose
That strode to the door and knocked,
And shattered the dream like a rose
Till the magical reverie rocked,
Splitting the shell? Who knows?

Yet this is a man we remember,
A brutal fact made immortal
By the very assault on that chamber,
By the very knock on that portal,
By the death of that marvelous slumber.

What was the business that brought him?
Was it a matter of money?
Did he hound the god who besought him
To eat of his milk and wild honey?
Did he pity the god when he caught him?

Or was he, too, trapped in his duty,
As the poet in his, lest both perish?
Was his hand the preserver of beauty,
His trespass the torment we cherish,
Mad glimpse of a glimmering city?

When the coarse Intruder was come,
Who let the Intruder pass
To that palace of opium,
That delicate dome of glass,
That irretrievable dome?

Must it come always so,
When the poet has found his escape
In a fugitive phrase, that the blow,
Blind as revenge or rape,
Lays his illusion low?

A heavy heel on the stone,
A heavy hand at the door,
And the dreamer sinks with a moan,
And the tower falls to the floor,
Leaving a fragment like bone.

Leaving a bone and a feather
Dabbled with blood from his heart.
The dream and the dreamer together,
The world and the poet apart,
And the pieces the world will gather,

Those pieces of pain the Destroyer
Will put under glass in a room,
Where the dusty drapes like a lawyer
Mumble their pompous doom,
And the guard falls asleep in the foyer.

Who was the man from Porlock?
Who stumbled on Kublai Khan?
Did he wear a wet little forelock?
Was he a slippery warlock?
What sort of man was this man?

Thoughts

Thoughts move in the mind
Like birds moving in air:
Some hop, and some are too heavy,
Too heavy to bear.

And one thought buries its beak
Deep in the warmth of the mind;
And one is afraid to speak;
And one is blind.

And one is forever shaken
By the world's noise and smoke;
And one will never awaken
The heart it broke.

The Word

I.

I, wandering in the Garden of the Word,
A trespasser in Paradise; say, rather,
An exile braving the precarious Sword,
The Edict of a formidable Father;
I, wandering in that splendour, nevertheless,
Intent upon the peril of the bough,
Found the proud fruit where it lay in the grass,
Heard the cold question, "Adam, where art thou?"
The grass grew thick and tangled round the fruit;
The fruit where it had fallen glowed as red
As when it fell; I touched it with my foot,
And felt the first fierce wonder, the first dread;
And in the grasses felt the green coils gliding,
And in the stillness, "Adam, where art thou hiding?"

II.

To sink my teeth into the sovereign flesh
Of the first syllable; to taste that truth
Still fragrant of its origin, still fresh
From the inquisitive folly of our youth;
To smell the jealous god upon its flower;
To find where hotly to the core had bitten
That godlike hunger holy for an hour;
Plainly to see the record it had written—
That is the stigma burned into my birth,
The debt inherited from a desperate dream
Whereof in lonely places of the earth
I seem at moments—suddenly I seem—
To touch, to taste, to smell a rapture taken
Out of my hand that leaves me flushed and shaken.

III.

Some day, perhaps, as cool, as unconfessed
As love or death or liquid shift of leaf,
Along with many a familiar guest,
Shall loom the stubborn answer to my grief.
I will not know it by its name or face,
Or by a way it has of being wise,
But only by a casual sense of grace
As quiet as a hand across the eyes.
I am a child dragged off to sullen sleep,
Still troubled by a piece he cannot fit
Into his picture-puzzle, nor can keep
A memory of the dream that fitted it.
I sleep, I wake; sleeping and waking, hear
The same bleak accusation, "Adam, where——?"

And this familiar earth whereunder
Soon the seed of grass will beat
Like a blind heart, until the secret thunder
Shakes at my feet—
This earth can only whisper over and over, can only
    repeat,
"Winter was sweet. . . . Spring is sweet. . . ."

As now against my mood and mind,
Against the heart that coldly closes,
Some alien mood, a buried heart as blind
As this that grows is,
Murmurs, insists, mounts fiercely, gathers and
    shouts like a great wind,
"There will be grass . . . and rain . . . and roses! . . ."

"But Man is dying! Man is dead
Of hunger," I cry out, "and hate!
Terror and pestilence and turmoil tread
Upon his face, who ate
Black dust in yesterday's hurried grave! Blood and
    tears still soak his bread!"
"The willows are early . . . the swallows will not be
    late. . . ."

They Told Me, Heraclitus . . .

For A. E. Housman

More than a poet passes
Out of the world of words,
Out of men's griefs and grasses,
Rain and bells and the birds:

A savage grace like satin
That gloves the panther's nail;
The pumice of pure Latin
To edge the English flail;

As classic and as cleric
As Horace when he sups;
As bibulous as Herrick
Drowned in his honeyed cups.

Not in our raucous time,
Not in our restless hour
Shall any poet rhyme
Such pathos and such power.

We shall no longer hear
In these amorphous days
That language like a spear,
That lean athletic phrase.

From our redundant verses,
From vapid and verbose,
Your stubborn skill coerces
The slow astringent rose:

The forehead's rigorous fillet,
The blossom on the cheek,
That, whether or not we will it,
Garlands our grief in Greek.

Now that your mouth the Reaper's
Impartial steel has kissed;
Now that among the Sleepers
You, too, sleep, wrist on wrist,—

Master, take these lines written
By love's impetuous art:
The minor lute-string smitten,
The hand upon the heart.

John Bunyan

You bluff British Dante in clout and in breeches,
And quite as intense as the sulphurous Tuscan,
You had not the heart for his fiery niches,
No stomach for torments refined and Etruscan.

Ho, sturdiest tinker of kettles and sinners
That ever blew trumpets in Malory's tongue!
You banqueted beggars delectable dinners;
The prince at your table stood up to your song.

The zeal of your exile stretched roots into Zion,
But Love ruled the Pilgrim and rang in the trumpet:
The love of mankind that could rage like a lion
To succour the vagrant, to solace the strumpet.

Lived ever a fellow with lust so celestial,
So human, whose hunger could eat good and evil;
With gusto angelic, with appetite bestial
Devour the World and the Flesh and the Devil?

Unworldly and vulgar, a dervish, a yokel,
As coarse as the tavern, as tender and shrewd,
Whose dream could transmute what was sordid and
        local,
And reconcile spirit and sense from their feud.

John Bunyan, John Bunyan, God's mercy attend
    you!
Forever and ever God's vision be yours!
Whom Love made a poet, that Love shall befriend
    you,
By virtue of which the bright Kingdom endures.

Elinor Wylie

These are not pen-and-ink prints, but a bird's,
Small and most unimaginable, that flew
From some far kingdom, fabulous with words,
And rested on this page a minute or two.
These are not interrupted by vague terror,
Nor hurried into unfamiliar flight:
The delicate pattern never ravels error;
The picture never snarls in tangled fright.
This is the jeweled bird of fire and ice;
Immortal Phoenix wrought of ice and fire,
With plumage smooth and lucent and precise,
With emerald claws and crest of cunning wire;
This is the princess; this the bird she cages
In a proud secret book with curious pages.

Writ in Water

For John Keats

Your name is writ in water; but what stone,
However brave it seems, and garlanded
With pomp, outlives the dull oblivion
It celebrates, the prince it puts to bed.
Your name is writ in water; but what urn
Of bronze is less brief than the lord it keeps,
Who, but for verses that set death at scorn,
Were colder than the castle where he sleeps.
No shift of wind, nor temporal malice, nor
Taste's weathercock that rides a giddy staff
Can taint the marble of that watery floor
Whereon the moon your restless epitaph
Forever writes, forever leaves unwritten—
The poem in suspense; the poet smitten.

II.

Your name is writ in water; but to write
A name in water is nobler than a name
Men cherish, or the moth, since both are light
As the small dust they worship, or the flame.
Never shall men betray you, being human,
And therefore hot with love a little while;
Nor shall you suffer any second woman
To feed your passion with some sugared guile.
Your name is writ in water, but it pours
Like blood from heart to heart, from sea to sea;
It drops red wine on gleaming corridors,
Trailing the wound of its divinity.
We face the Perilous Foam, the Silent Peak;
We find a name there, but we cannot speak.

Thunderbox

The thunder makes the earth his sounding-board;
She echoes back his cloud—and that is thunder.
Without her hills no thunder could be heard;
Her sultry bosom nests the thunderbird,
The terror of whose beak she trembles under.

Earth, make of me your thunderbox, your drum!
Hammer your tumults on my heart, and hammer
Your wings and winds, bright water and honeycomb,
Your lights and shadows and green secret clamour
Dimly surmised by the spirit's tympanum.

And pound your people deep into my side,
Like a dear wound—the folly and the wonder,
The bitterness, the passion and the pride,
Thoughts that drag down, dreams that will not stay
        under—
Pound them against my senses like a tide!

I sicken of private verses and the sound
Of metered heart-throbs, the pathetic plunder
Of self. I press my ear against your ground;
I drink your strength; I am a strength unbound;
I am a trumpet bright with beating thunder!

More Than Bread

There are hungers that cannot be fed
With a loaf of bread,
But only with love, hard as hate,
Implacable on a plate.

You must drive a plow of love, like steel,
Deep into the sullen heart,
Churning up secret sour hatreds that eat at the heart
Until it is only a hollow shell;
Sick dreads and slimy hypocrisies that smell
To heaven let not the heart conceal:
Press your heel on the plow, bear down, rend them
     apart,
Stamp them like snakes under your heel!

The earth must have her way with these,
And the wind and the sun and the tolerant rain and
     the slow
Soft fall of snow:
Those dread hates will dung lilies and cabbages,
     those foul hypocrisies
Will flush into candid acacia trees;
Those fears
Inform bold apples and blunt yellow pears.

Bread is not enough;
No matter how bland
In the fullness thereof,
We remain ill-fed.
We are weak;
We can hardly stand;
We can scarcely speak.
The iron strength of love must keep a hand
In us, the stubborn love,
As clear as light, as clean as wind, and stronger
Than any hunger.

Splendour of Words

What virtue lingers in the sullen splendour
Of words! How can we covet words too highly!
The secret of some words will not surrender
To bribes or battles, that would step as shyly
As speckled young deer toward an outstretched hand
To nuzzle there with a delicious tingle
That stops the heart for breath; and some words stand
With high proud nostrils, that would sooner strangle
Than budge an inch of their uneasiness;
And some as ripe as fruit sunned in the south,
Fragrant with gold and eager to possess
A poet's passionate blood, his burning mouth;
And seldom, if at all, that perilous rhyme,
That ragged page ripped from the promptbook of
    Time!

We have our own dark way of saying things,
And they have theirs.
We grudge them not their flights, their flashing
  wings,
Their difficult glories and their steep despairs,
Knowing how brief a song it is that sings
Equally to all hearts, all ears.

We only know the singing must be made
Out of our common grief,
As pure as light, as palpable as shade,
As definite as fruit or falling leaf;
We only know that on our hearts at length is laid
That song, and it is brief.

To the Poets Who Fly Left

They fret, they sweat, they frown,
Insist that so we do;
They shout Catullus down,
Shout Keats down, too.

They sneer, they howl, they snort,
Insist that so we sing;
Yet Frost can still report
The snow, the spring.

They stamp, they gnash, they bray,
They madden and they mock;
The Hawk of Monterey
Still reads his rock.

Clearly the God

Clearly the god dwells in a cloud;
His voice booms from a fog-bound ship.
Sovereign, unseeable and proud,
Truth perches on his fingertip.

The moon that wets our hands and feet
Is of some secret moon the shadow;
It rubs the cherries chilly-sweet,
Bruises our mouths in the milky meadow.

We name with little names the things
Which parrot neatly, name for name.
We seldom hear the fiery wings;
We seldom see the flame.

Lesser Creature

After the rain is over,
The roof steams in the sun;
The bee with his golden muzzle in clover
Finds it all one.

It is ourselves that divide
The sun from the rush of rain,
The ebb of passion from the full tide,
Pleasure from pain.

Not so the lesser creature
That lives in a single breath,
That never imputes to the truth of nature
The falsehood of death.

Cold

Out of the world I went,
Into a wood where snow
Bowed the sky and bent
Larch and hemlock low.

No shape moved, no sound
Swept in hushed rebuke
Of snow to snowy ground;
No blue shadow shook.

Not even my breath could blur
That quiet cloud of trees,
That house carved from white air,
That cavern of cold peace.

April the Shulamite

Intense and timid, April stammers her story
Again, as last year; she, the Shulamite,
Stuttering of turtles and the brutal glory
Of lust and the brilliant idiom of light;
Blurting out breathless news of floods and flowers,
Shambles of pain and starry incidents
Under a stone still steaming with sweet showers,
And doves that gurgle golden indolence.
She is the same as when that beautiful Jew,
Whose Song shook like a god in mortal fever,
Stood in the tents of Kedar or walked the dew
Of David's vineyard where the blue grapes shiver;
She is the same as when that Song was new;
That Song will be the same forever and ever.

Spring Has Cold Hands

Always the restless young whose eyes are hot
Pluck at the heels of Winter and plague his ears
With questions about Spring, as like as not,
And then when April wistfully appears
From nowhere, out of breath, a hunted thing,
Still wet with snow, and quite the worse for mud,
The young cry out, "Can we believe this Spring
Whose cold hands break our hearts and freeze our
    blood?"
Only the old who dream the Song of Songs
By a slow blaze at night, and all alone;
Only the old whom every weather wrongs,
Who soon will sleep, and softly, under stone:
These only with old eyes can see, can feel
The faint wing fumbling at the muddy heel.

Adolescence

When the young year, half-woman, half-child,
For the first time puts up her hair,
The heart in her side strikes sharp and wild;
Her breast is a pointed little pear.

She is fearful of being too late,
And ashamed her haste may make her too soon;
She is torn between hope and the whisper of fate;
She walks with small steps under the moon.

She looks behind her; she hurries along,
Head high, face flushed, hands cold, pretending
She does not envy the vivid throng,
Afraid to begin, afraid of the ending.

She is proud and lonely and stubborn and slight;
She is troubled by something; she cannot speak;
She is changed; she is not the same; something tight
Twists in her flesh like a secret beak.

No use to go back now. This will never
Leave you alone, this burden of flame.
You have walked out too far. There are lights on the
    river.
Your breath comes quick. You are not the same.

Obit

Who knows if any song we sing
Will long survive its buried spring,
Or patience bring again to light
The casual rhyme our ashes write.

This heart we finger for a phrase
Can never hear the shout of praise,
Nor find beneath the fallen stone
The critic's dust unlike its own.

And even these dull words were said
By other singers done and dead,
Whose mossy obits our nails scratch
To flicker on a blowing match.

Dark Treason

More savage, more insistent even
Than hunger, safety, hope or reason,
The poet and his kind are driven
By an instinct dark as treason:

A faith as furious and blind,
A secret and a terrible force
Flog the poet and his kind
Like the salmon to his source,

Like the lemming to his doom,
Like the locust to his burning,
Back into the difficult womb,
Fierce and punctual returning;

Back in spite of rock and torrent,
Tide and turmoil, fire and furrow;
Back into the quiet current,
Or death as frugal as an arrow;

Back against the stubborn fury
Driving each to plant his hunger
Like a bone that he must bury,
Like a bone of golden anger;

Like the salmon to his breeding,
Like the locust, like the lemming,
Back in spite of bruise and bleeding,
Sudden torch or seas gleaming.

So the poet shares his valour
With these three, his quest and quarrel,
Tasting in one flash of failure
Glory longer than the laurel.

This Consequence

This consequence
Of mind and sense,
This little poem naked out of nothing;
This ordered dust
Adorn I must
With linen of delight, with noble clothing.

I cannot leave
This fugitive,
This foundling of an accidental slumber;
This brightness wrought
By measured thought
Out of some agony we do not remember.

No bell, no horn
Hail this prince born,
No pillow hushes, no soft palms applaud;
Quiet he comes
Like dead-march drums,
His father a vagabond, his mother a bawd.

O brief escape,
O starry shape
Bright in the reeds, O freight more fine than Moses!
Pathetic lamb,
Whose sire I am,
Lo, I will deck your bones with rags of roses!

That shining whore,
The world, which bore
Your beauty and my hope in one womb sheltered;
Whose belly was
A pleasant place—
Though she disowns her child, I have not altered.

Cassandra Again

He shrieks out, being driven,
Wild truths he cannot know.
They strike him down unshriven;
He hardly feels the blow;
His eyes still glow.

Or, if his god forsake him,
They let him live instead;
They tie him up and make him
Repeat the things he said.
They spit upon his head;

Or drag him to the gateway
With laughter loud and coarse,
And stone him there, and straightway,
Too reckless for remorse,
They open to the Horse.

Archeological Episode

I

They found a daughter of Pharaoh in her case
Of incorruptible wood; she looked the same
As when they set the Asp upon her face,
Her face still feverish with an inner flame.
They tell that when they scraped away the mud
Which had seeped in from the recurrent Nile
Her eyes still blazed a Princess of the Blood,
Immortal scorn still flashed a bitter smile.
And then like some strange star that claws the night
Almost wide open enough for the moon to fall
Before it falls itself in a rain of light
And turns to ashes on some farmer's wall,
This daughter of the Pharaohs, so they say,
In a brief shock of brilliance burned away.

II.

And I, hearing these curious tidings spoken,
And mindful of a princess long forgotten,
Unreasonably marvelled by what token
Of gold or glass, what bands of musky cotton,
What poignant little oars on little ships
Loaded with little jars of wine and bread—
By how much could her thirst attend her lips?
How could these things please her imperious head?
Pathetic passion against death, poor hope
Huddling in darkness, haughty and infirm,
What purpose could you serve beyond the scope
Of Time's ambiguous patience, and the worm?
And yet there rose an outcry in the night,
And yet men saw a bloom of blinding light!

Love Knowing Best

Love will never be found
By searching here and there;
Love is all around,
Nowhere, and everywhere,
And nowhere bound.

Love will never come
To greedy cry or touch.
It will desert the home
That loves it overmuch,
And there are such.

Love will never let rest
The heart that once has known it;
Nor leave at peace the breast
That would disown it,
Love knowing best.

Medusa Twice

I have come back from gazing
On love that gasps for breath :
I watched the eyeballs glazing
With the Medusa Death.

I knew that love would never
Await another year
The break-up of the river,
The first green spear.

I have come back as old
As Death, as cold as ice :
I saw the snakes unfold;
I faced Medusa twice.

The Poet Pursues His Dream

The poet pursues his dream
When the others are talking,
And makes the whole world seem
His shadow walking.

The poet hunts his hope,
His blinding vision,
Proud as the antelope,
Cold as derision.

The poet stalks his heart
Like a wild bird hiding,
Until he hears, with a start,
Great wings riding.

Mocked by that harsh whirring,
Fouled with the swamp's mire,
He turns to find his heart purring
By his own hearthfire!

Yet Out of Time

Day follows day in glassy sequence moving
Like convicts in a lockstep, each the same
Since Adam made a heavy calendar, proving
His exile and our shame.

As when Macbeth, trapped in a round of sorrow,
Pacing his cell the world, dragging its chain,
Beat bloody fists against tomorrow's tomorrow,
Beat bloody fists in vain.

Time is our turnkey, whether or not we know it,
Man's dreadful Frankenstein, his mortal mime
To clock him slave, to measure him a poet
With ball and chain of rhyme.

Yet out of Time, time past and time to come,
The poet builds against Time's ponderous curse
His anger like a delicate little bomb
To explode the universe.

And Who Can Say

And who can say when the horse with wings
Will rub his nose in your hand?
I have seen him canter by queens and kings;
I have seen him stop and stand
By a fool whose pockets bulged stupid things
Like stones and strings.

I have seen him lower his glowing head
And paw the stubborn ground
And whinny as sweet, as daintily tread
As any mare to be found,
And turn from clover to eat the bread
Of a beggar, instead.

And who can say when that ringing hoof
Will set one man apart,
And make a poet-prince of an oaf
Who never had heard of art,
And leave us staring at the starry proof
On some humble roof?

Simple Music

I will not follow any piper,
Nor jig to any of his piping.
I have seen pipers come and go,
Heard the dancing and the clapping,
And after the dancing and the clapping,
What was left to show—

A heel, perhaps, a buckle or two,
Maybe a feather, maybe a button,
The marks of teeth in a muddy apple,
All this swept up and soon forgotten,
And the sad little dancers quite forgotten,
Like a button, a rotten apple.

I will follow my heart's unpopular fashion,
Pluck my song to the blood's old measure,
Dance to my own pipe, come what will,
Damn private gain and public pleasure,
Knowing how Time's hard truth must treasure
The simple music still.

The Towers of New York

There was a Tower
In the land of Shinar
That flashed for an hour
And fell like a star:
There was a Tower and the babbling of many
tongues—and none of these are.

Are your towers as well
The sick fruit of fable?
A doomed citadel?
A luxurious stable?
O City, my City, must you also blaze and burn out
like a Babel?

We have decked you with mountains
Of dreams and despairs,
With stone-and-steel fountains,
With sun-trampling prayers—
We have gouged the moon out, we have marched to
the stars on white stairs!

We have filled you with people,
Inflamed you with power:
O remember the Steeple
That flashed for an hour
And fell like a star in Shinar—and that was a beau-
tiful Tower.

O my City, my City,
So fierce in your pride,
Be fierce in your pity:
For mountains can slide,
And a dream can keep them from falling—and
  dreams without pity have died.

The City

How shall I trap you into a poem who are
Too vast for any verses to contain?
What box is big enough to hold a star
Or cage a hurricane?

How shall I lure you into the wordy lime?
How dig the pit with phrase and metaphor?
What stanza is tight enough, what ruse of rhyme
Strong enough for a door?

Love snarling and clawing can at length be tamed
Into a sullen routine, and also hate;
But you, whose beauty and terror cannot be named,
Heart's hunger alone must bait:

Only the savage hunger of the heart,
Spitted upon a verb like some young sheep,
Can coax you into the corral of art
And lull your hunger to sleep.

Strange Mother

Nature bears no grievance; Nature cherishes
No grudge; she neither loves nor hates; she neither
Forgets nor remembers the leopard, the leaf that
  perishes.
She is a strange and terrible mother.
(But, such as she is, she is ours; we have no other.)

We only, of all her issue, and scarcely the lordliest
To bawl our bloody exits out of her luxurious
  womb—
We, and we only, question, accuse; we feed in our
  breast
A sulky anger at birth, a bitterness we carry into the
  tomb.
(We frighten ourselves with shadows in an empty
  room.)

There are no regrets, no elegies in Nature;
She has no use for graveyards; she cannot weep
  there;
Leopard or leaf in dying distort no feature;
Death buries in her heart a bone to keep there.
(Even her fretful man-child finally falls asleep
  there.)

A Night in Spring

Our servant, out on his moon-washed stone,
Rubs his knife to an edge as sharp
As any the hand of a man could hone
To scrape the scales of a golden carp.

The scales fly up in a golden shower,
And I think how beautiful a thing
God will devise and man devour
On a quiet moon-washed night of spring.

The Frightened Ones

But never inquire
Too closely of these
That, housed in the briar,
Will come by degrees
To rock at your fire,
To sleep at your knees.

For they are the frightened,
The wild ones that fled,
Whose heavy hearts tightened
To shut out their dead,
Whose lips never lightened
Their nightmare of dread.

They ran from the pity
Of angels; they ran
From a beautiful city
And the terror of man,
From conscience and duty,
From cannot and can.

They ran from a Garden
They hated because
The trees bore a Burden,
The fruit reeked of Laws;
They rushed from the Pardon
That begged them to pause.

Reach never a hand;
Say never a word
To this alien band,
To the fugitive bird
Whose eyes understand
What the ears have heard.

Caress them—they're gone;
Console them—they've vanished.
They are best left alone
To startle, astonished,
From behind the stone
Where they stare, self-banished.

So never inquire
Too closely of these
That, housed in the briar,
Will come by degrees
To rock at your fire,
To sleep at your knees.

The Multitude

How can the soul bear it?
How can there be any more room
For a man or a woman to share it
Till the noisy morning of doom?

There are so many now, so many,
Since they plugged the first proud nostrils with mud,
Since they pinned down the eyes with a penny
And wiped away the blood.

How can a man be private?
How can a prince be alone?
How can the spirit survive it,
Mixed with the multitude under stone?

Hospitable Earth

Dying is a lonely thing,
And a lonely thing is the being born.
But Death, though it were a king,
Is loud and public as a circus horn.

Death is something we do
To people, an indignity we heap
Upon the dead, Gentile or Jew,
Piled in a sorry promiscuous sleep.

Death is something the patient earth
Endures at our hands; nevertheless
Her enormous courtesy gives worth
To the sordid flesh in sudden grass.

Her hospitality rejects nothing
Of our nothingness, but clothes
The holes we dig in her heart with clothing
Of sunny wind and dew and the dropping rose.

Having No Wisdom

The water pimples up under the wind;
Roughens up in gooseflesh under that flail;
The gust bites blue where the feathers are thinned
On the throat of the quail.

The North plows blue in the puckered fur
Of beaver and rat and gleaming otter;
Electric blue flashes the kingfisher;
Blue flashes the water.

These furry things, these flying things
Accept the shrill assault and shape it
To thicken their coats, to curve their wings,
And not to escape it.

Having no wisdom beyond their need,
Uncumbered with a sense of terror,
They test their skins, they tune their speed,
They make a blunt mirror

Of peril (which humans hardly care to)
Where Death sits naked and precise,
And face the Death that shines, and dare to
Endure it twice.

Alien

The river shimmered and swirled and bloomed like
    oil
And eddied blue and rose among the weeds;
The lithe trout lashed the eddies to a boil;
The coot clanked musically in the reeds.

A flashing trout shook peacock scales in light;
The minnow leaned on rays that ran forever;
Swallow and swift darted from dark to bright;
The sun shifted: a hush fell on the river.

Only the mayflies flickered; only the tide
Of fullness draining out of the deep heart; only
The colours and the clamours that subside;
And someone foreign to this peace, and lonely.

Trampled Ground

Can we trample the heart
As we trample the ground?
Plow it apart?
Pull it around?
Pile it up into a mound?
Shovel it into a cart?

Is the heart more hard
Than the iron earth?
Less apt to be scarred
For a stubborn birth
Than April, astringently starred
Against the heart's dearth?

Can the heart put on leaves,
Can the heart bud
Out of the grief it grieves,
Out of heart's blood,
One cold small cup that retrieves
The snow, the mud?

Where is the share to furrow?
Where is the steel?
What plowman's compassionate harrow,
What hand, what heel
Can trample the heart? What arrow
Can this heart feel?

Even If the Singer

The end is not yet;
There are other poems to be made:
Proud songs to fret
The heart that has too long delayed;
Brave songs to set
At peace the mind that feels afraid.

It is far from finished.
Never you fear, never you mind
The need undiminished
In a world grown bitter and blind;
The voice has not vanished,
Though the singer has been left behind.

Though the dead poet lies
Sprawled out obscenely in broad air,
Staring up at the flies
Loud in his hair—
The song never dies,
Even if the singer has gone elsewhere.

Ambiguous Child

This is hardly a matter
For burning punk and papers;
Something beside the teeth can chatter
And cut up capers.

Nor can a priest propitiate
The hooded eyes of fear,
Nor starry chart, though it come straight
From the astrologer.

This is the curse inherited
From Adam's angry seed,
That, having seen a bullock bled,
Would watch a brother bleed.

This is the double curse we bear
Twinned in one turbulent yolk,
That love and hate will blandly wear
Each the other's cloak.

Wherefore, bedevilled by our love,
Or by our hate beguiled,
We know not which is father of
The bright ambiguous child.

Wherefore we go forever torn
By our blind hearts in two,
Finding in love a lance of scorn
Ready to run us through;

Finding in hate a savage glow
Of strength to match our need :
And bleeding under the same blow
That makes our brother bleed.

The Snail

Regard the snail,
That in a narrow room
Inhabits both
His tower and his tomb.

His hollow house,
Poised like a sculptured wave,
Becomes at once
His fortress and his grave.

To creep, while Time
Whirls like a maniac!
To carry Death
Softly upon my back!

To walk entombed
Within my pearly scorn,
Not naked dead,
Not blind and naked born!

This ponderous inch,
Where Life and Death go twinned,
Claims vaster space
Than the impulsive wind.

Ah, sovereign yet,
Though men and planets reel!
Ah, undelayed
Beneath the hasty heel!

Derricks and Rainbows

Horizons cannot nourish me,
Nor dullness in a deacon's hat;
No mathematical certainty
Ever clothed my bones with fat.

I'd rather lick the empty cup
That John Keats poured his porridge in
Than wear a cutaway and sup
With sober folk on terrapin.

I know a derrick excavates
A culvert, tears a hill in two:
It is as real as addled pates;
It does the work that derricks do.

It lifts a mountain by the hair;
It even cracks a mountain's spine;
And yet I know a ghost of air,
Than gossamer less firm, more fine,

Less actual than light or cloud,
Child of the drenched and dripping sky,
The hostage given man by God
That man might see him better by;

A thing as friendly and remote,
That sets a bridge between them both,
That shakes a man, that grips his throat,
That binds God by the rainbow oath.

The derrick splits earth wide apart;
The derrick bites a mountain through;
The rainbow raises up the heart,
Which derricks want the strength to do.

Poet and Spider

The spider labours long;
Out of his naked belly, minute by minute,
He builds his patient song:
Hope is in it,
Hunger is in it,
Hate is in it—
His house is strong.

The spider spins and spins,
And knows that nothing under the sunny sky
Is worth a pair of pins
Unless a fly,
A well-plushed fly,
A well-picked fly
Ends what he begins.

Poet and spider as well,
If they be honest, from their hot bowels spin it
Each his airy citadel:
Hope is in it,
Hunger is in it,
Heaven is in it—
And enough of hell.

A poem is like a tree
Heavy with fruit,
Sucking a slow eternity
Up through its root.

I Am Poetry

I am Poetry.
I am as old as yesterday.
I am as young as tomorrow.
I am the servant of anguish.
I am the antidote to despair.
I am the grayness of grief.
I am the green of hope.
I am the vessel of courage.
I am the hunger for God.

I am Poetry.
I comfort the sick.
I solace the dying.
I console the bereaved.
I carry a torch of truth.
I light up the dark places.
Against cruelty and corruption
I cry out with a terrible voice;
No tyranny can survive it.

I am Poetry.
I am the spirit of spring.
I am the passion for beauty.
In the bitterness of winter
I bring you the birds
And the recurrent miracle of bloom.
I am the summer evenings and the stars,
And the husky whisperings in the park.
I am the Song of Songs.

I am Poetry.
I boast a noble lineage.
I was the Spirit brooding over the face of the waters.
I was the Word.
I was the divine torment in the mind of the Creator
That cried out for light.
I sang with the Morning Stars.
I breathed the dream of God into the soul of man.
I made a world.

I am Poetry.
You will find me everywhere.
I am equally at home
In the castle of a king
Or the hut of a peasant.
I am the pride of imagination
And the power of dream.
I sustain the battle.
I will not let you down.

I am Poetry.
Once upon a time
The people called on my name
To prosper their crops,
To make their vines heavy,
To fatten their flocks.
In my name they invoked
The sun and the wind
To give them good voyagings.

I am Poetry.
Call me, and I will come.
I will answer your need.
I will open your eyes
To the glory in the commonplace.
Are you lonely?
I will companion you.
Are you broken?
I will make you whole.

I am Poetry.
Give me a chance,
And I will help you.
When your little world crumbles
I will stand like a mountain.
When you choke up with joy
I will be your voice.
When you hesitate
I will be your trumpet.

I am Poetry.
No matter who you are,
I have a message for you.
I have stormed Bastilles.
And I have given the captive
A Song of Zion.
I have sinewed the hand
Of the hero in battle.
I have heartened a people.

I am Poetry.
I am not a matter of correct scansion.
I am not a melodious hocus-pocus
Enunciated softly into a vacuum.
Against the tooth and treachery of time
I preserve the splendour of the world.
I am your memory.
I am the most beautiful way of remembering
What it would impoverish you to forget.

I am Poetry.
I write the nation's songs.
I write the history
That is bigger than names and dates.
I write the legends
That laugh at cold facts
And live beyond them.
I confer on time
The dignity of timelessness.

I am Poetry.
Ask David about me,
And he will tell you.
Ask Prince and Prophet.
Ask Greek and Roman.
Ask Lincoln weeping
Alone at midnight.
Ask the men in the mud
And filth of Flanders.

I am Poetry.
And I am the vision
Without which the people perish.
I am more than bread.
I cannot be bought.
I have never gone off the gold standard.
I am eternal value.
I am the Company of the Spirit.
I have been paying dividends since the first week of
      Genesis.

I am Poetry.
I am your immortal birthright.
Without me life is drab.
Without me life is dangerous.
Why do you neglect me?
Why do you starve your poets,
Who lift up your hearts,
Who redeem from decay
The visitations of the divinity in man?

I am Poetry.
I confront you with Keats
Coughing his life away
When he had only just started to sing.
I accuse you with Poe,
Hounded by debt,
Driven by poverty and hunger
To death in a charity ward
Like a common drunkard.

I am Poetry.
I am the candid mirror of the present,
And I am the mirror of the gigantic dooms
Which tomorrow casts upon today.
I am the clear meaning
In the heat and the tumult.
I am the difference between
A full life and a crowded existence.
I am the shadow of a great rock in a weary land.

I am Poetry.
I am taller than the Empire State Building,
Which is only a little poem in steel and stone.
I am longer than the George Washington Bridge,
For I bind the poles of the earth together
With a simple song.
I am stronger than the derrick that scoops up a
     mountain.
I lift the heavy heart
With a rainbow or a leaf.

AP

A